On The Road To Bethlehem

Steven Harder wrote this collection of Nativity songs when he was 16 years old. He had won two local carol competitions, and had been persuaded not to enter for a third year. However, Steven's music teacher at the time encouraged him to write some new carols anyway, despite not being able to enter the competition.

This delightful collection of five songs, entitled **On The Road To Bethlehem**, was written as a result of that encouragement. Steven spent six weeks of his summer holiday composing the songs.

Steven Harder is now a music teacher. He writes:

"I hope that this short cycle of songs will be sung and enjoyed by schools, junior choirs, churches etc. The 10-minute length should be ideal where only a limited time is available during concerts. **On The Road To Bethlehem** provides an enjoyable celebration of the Christmas story and is fun to sing, and will still leave time for other musical contributions to a Christmas concert.

"The tape will make learning of the songs very easy indeed, if played to pupils during art etc. Alternatively, should you wish to approach the songs in the traditional manner, the Pupil's Book contains the choir parts, in addition to the song words and narration."

Alison Hedger

On The Road To Bethlehem

by Steven Harder
Arranged and Edited by Alison Hedger

A cycle of five songs retelling the Nativity story.
For voices (some two-part work) and piano accompaniment.

Duration approx. 10 mins.

For children aged 9 years and over.
Key Stages 2 + 3

TEACHER'S BOOK
Complete with the short narration and piano accompaniment, including chord symbols.

SONGS

1. The Angel's Message
2. On The Road To Bethlehem
3. No Room At The Inn
4. Mary's Lullaby*
5. Come Follow The Star*

* These songs have some optional second parts

The Pupil's Book, Order No. GA10645, contains the choir parts, song words and narration.

A matching tape cassette of the music for rehearsals and performances is also available,
Order No. GA10812, side A with vocals included and side B with vocals omitted.

Order No. GA10637
ISBN 0-7119-3458-4

THE ANGEL'S MESSAGE

E♭ Gm Cm Fm7 G7
His fa - vour, and you shall have His child. The
Cm Fm B♭ E♭ Fm7 B♭7
ba - by will be the Son of God, and o'er us all shall
crescendo
E♭ Fm G Cm B♭ A♭ Cm
reign. He'll be the King of Is - ra - el, Je -
crescendo
Fm7 G7 Cm CHORUS f Fm7 G7
- sus shall be His name. He'll be the King of all cre -
f f

-a - tion, the One and on - ly Je - sus Christ He'll be the
way un - to sal - va - tion. He'll be King of Is - ra -
- el."
rit.
f
ff

 Before the birth of Jesus, a decree went out that everyone should be registered in their own city. So Mary and Joseph set out on the long journey to Bethlehem.

SONG 2 — ON THE ROAD TO BETHLEHEM

F   G♭   F   mp Gm   C
on.
3. Ma - ry is sit - ting on the
Am   Dm   Gm   C7   F
back of a don - key with Jo - seph right there by her side.
Gm   C   Am   Dm   G
Gid - dy-up don - key, they've got to keep mov - ing, there's still a long way to ride.
C   mf F   Cm7   F7
4. Move a - long with all haste, for there

is no time to waste. Jo - seph and Ma - ry
are tra - vel - ling on. Jo - seph and
Ma - ry are tra - vel - ling on.
shake?

SONG 3   # NO ROOM AT THE INN

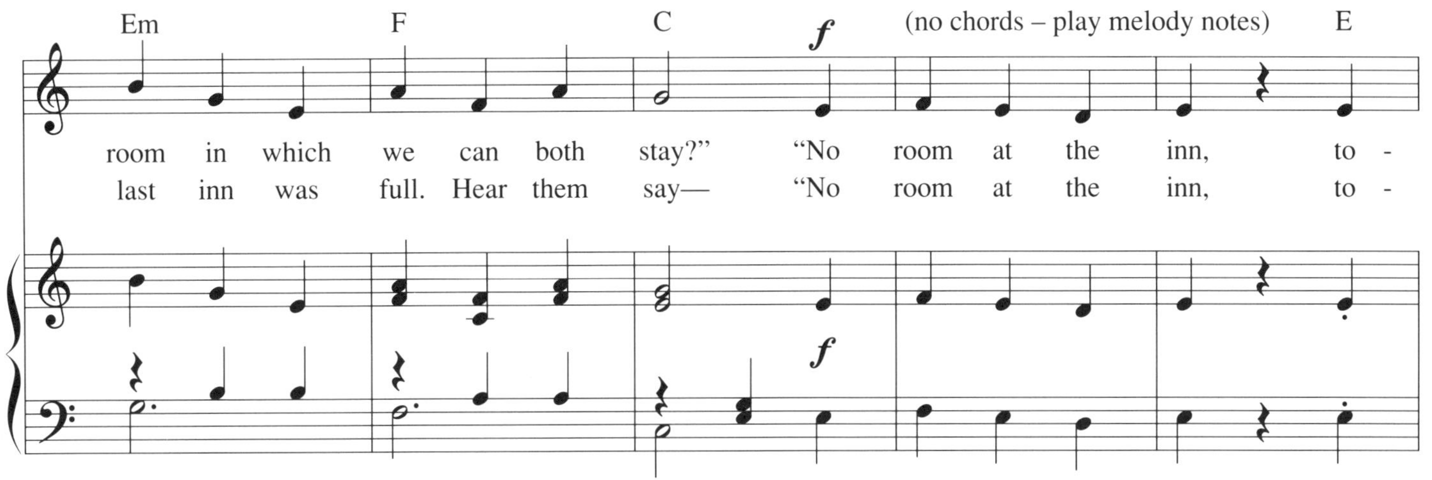

Em
F
C
f
(no chords – play melody notes)
E
room in which we can both stay?" "No room at the inn, to -
last inn was full. Hear them say— "No room at the inn, to -

First time
Am
day."
mf
3

mp
3

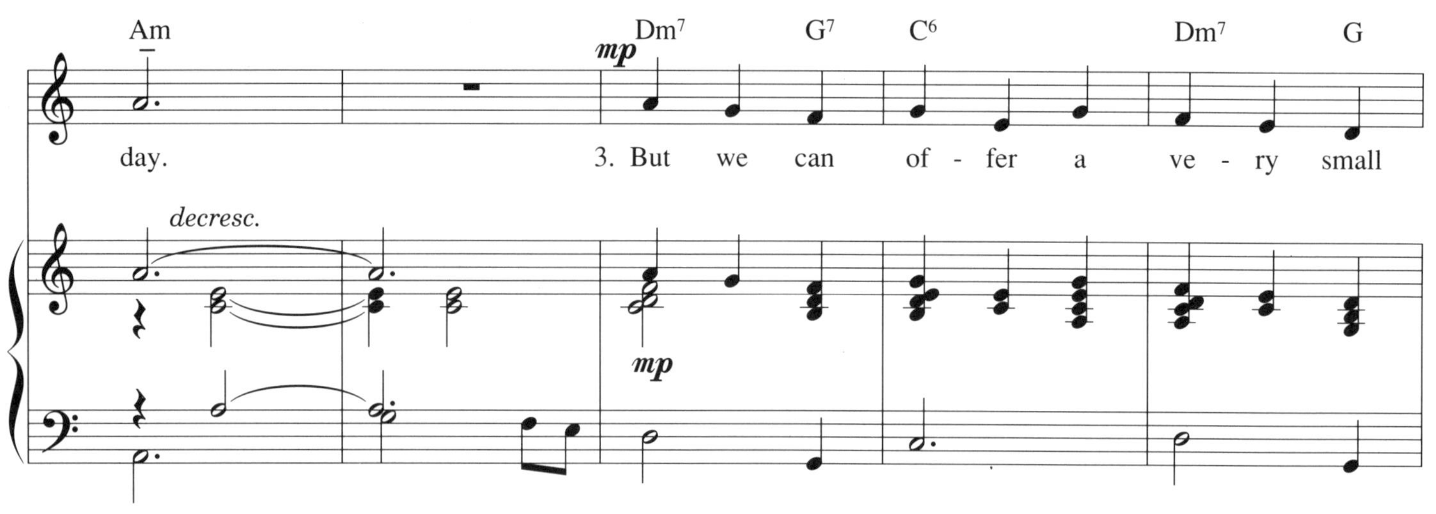

Am
mp   Dm7   G7   C6   Dm7   G
day.
decresc.
mp
3. But we can of - fer a ve - ry small

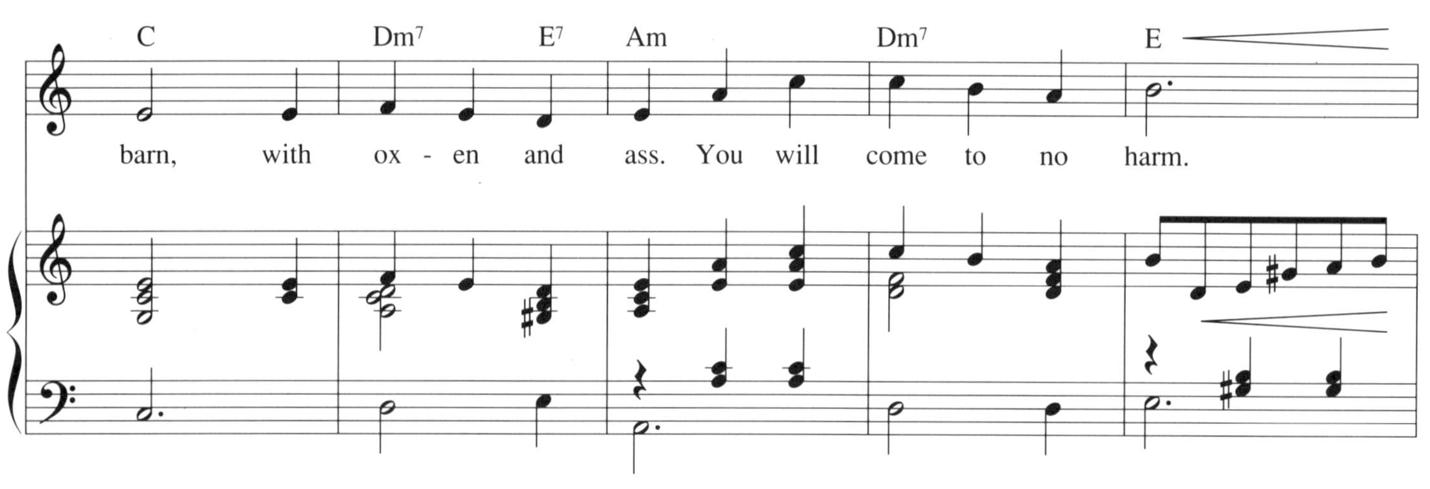

C   Dm7   E7   Am   Dm7   E
barn, with ox - en and ass. You will come to no harm.

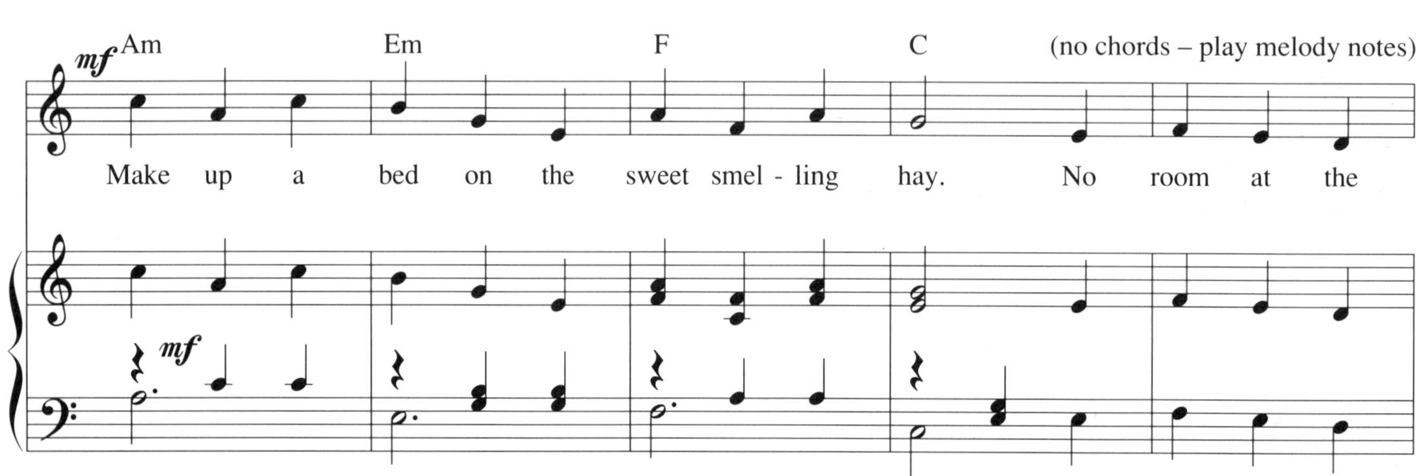

mf Am   Em   F   C   (no chords – play melody notes)
Make up a bed on the sweet smel - ling hay. No room at the
mf

E
Am
E^add♮6
mf
inn,
to - day.
To -
mf
3

Am
E^add♮6
mf
Am
- day,
to - day,
mf
3
mf

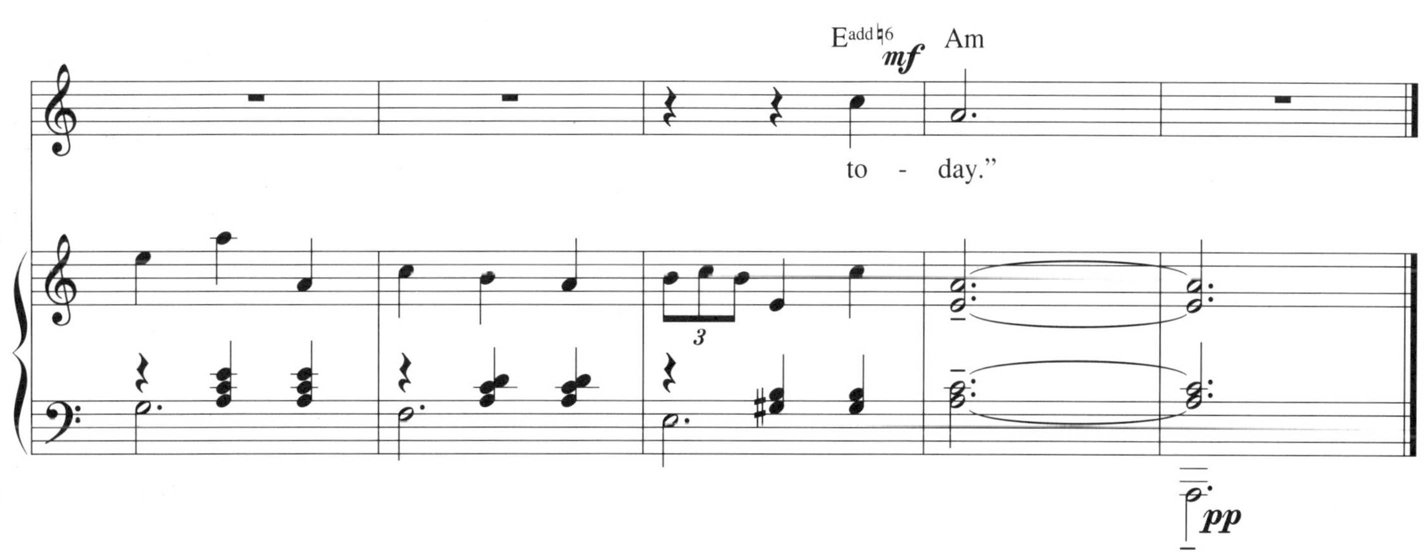

E^add♮6
mf
Am
to - day."
3
pp

SONG 4 MARY'S LULLABY

(Some two-part singing)

E♭
A♭
E♭
B♭7   div.
safe 'til the morn - ing light, my ba - by. Hush now, be still, lul - la -
E♭
B♭m7
mp
E♭7
by.
3. Rest in your man - ger of
mp
A♭
Fm
B♭m7
E♭7
soft warm hay, ox - en and ass by your
cresc.

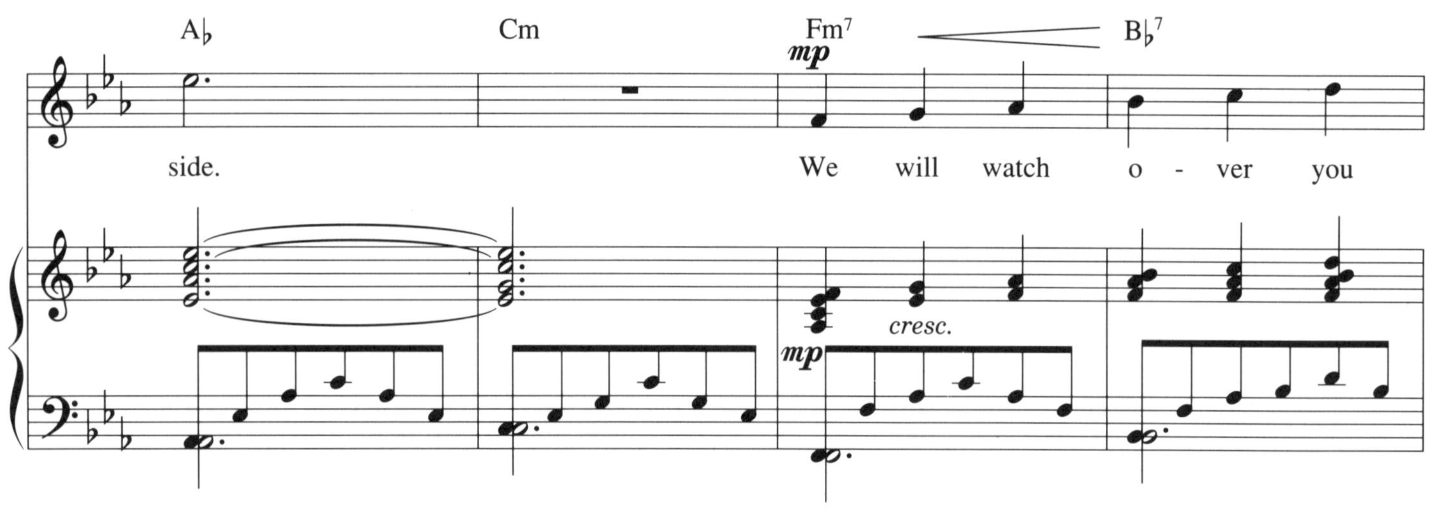

Ab
Cm
Fm7
Bb7
mp
side.
We will watch o - ver you
cresc.
mp

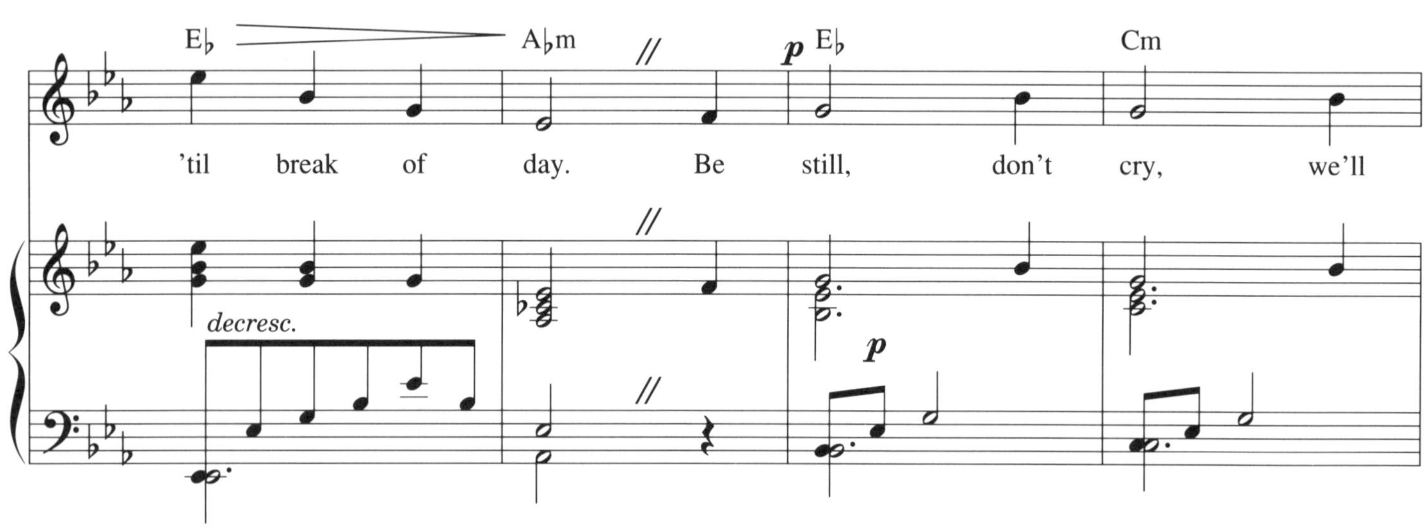

Eb
Abm
p Eb
Cm
'til break of day.
Be still, don't cry, we'll
decresc.
p

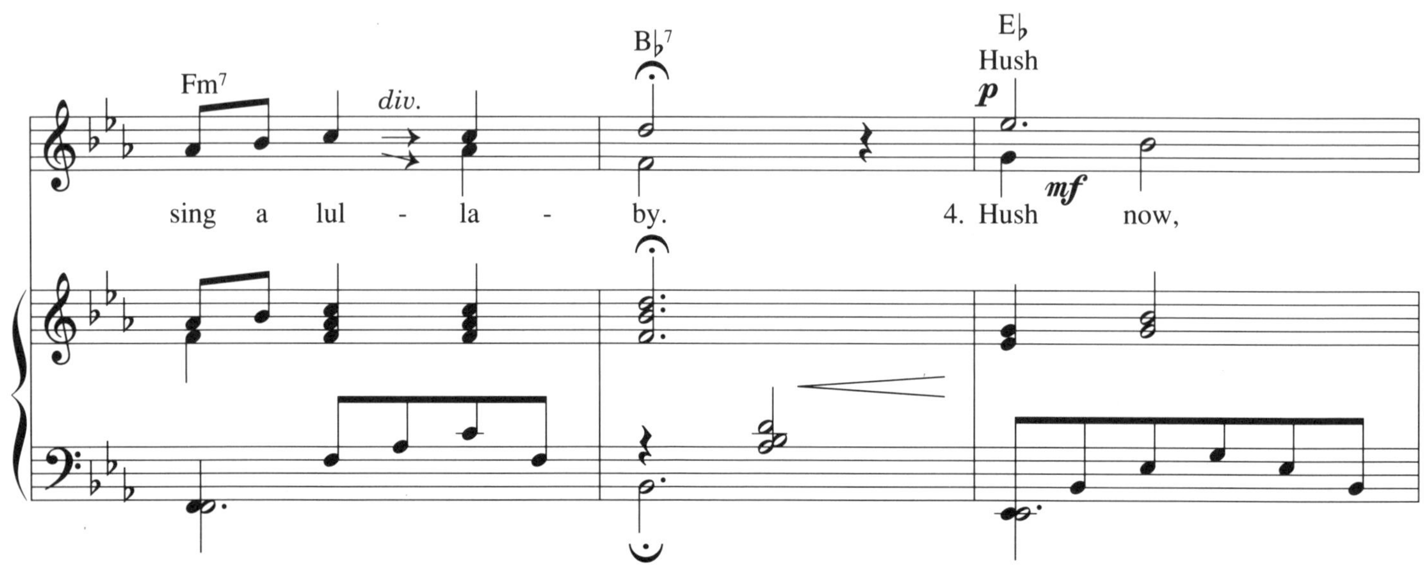

Fm7
div.
Bb7
Eb
Hush
p
sing a lul - la - by.
4. Hush now,
mf

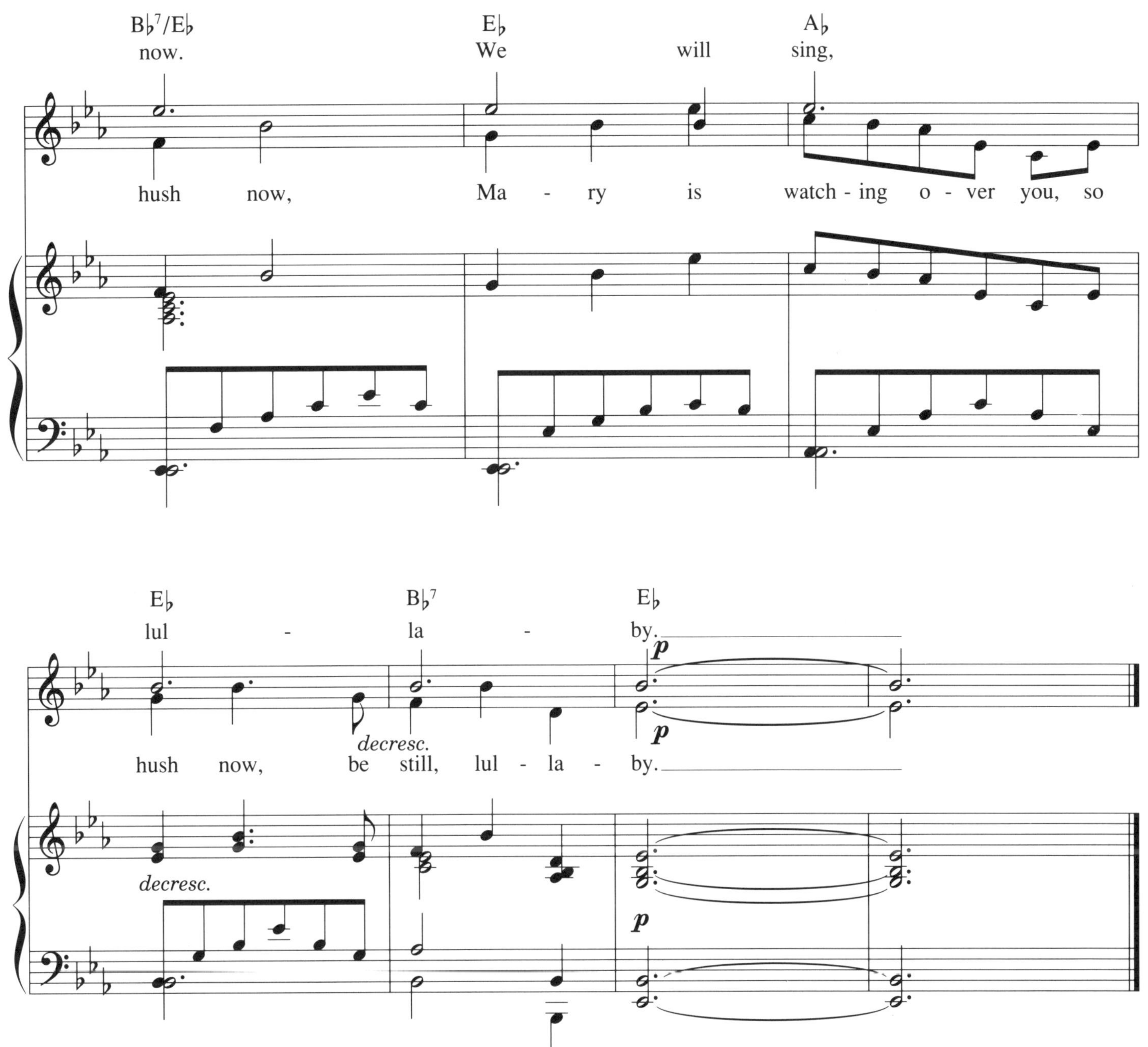

B♭7/E♭
now.
We will
E♭
A♭
sing,
hush now,
Ma - ry is
watch - ing o - ver you, so
E♭
B♭7
E♭
lul - la - by.
p
p
decresc.
hush now,
be still, lul - la - by.
decresc.
p
p

SONG 5

COME FOLLOW THE STAR

(Some optional two-part singing)

heaven a - bove ap - peared a won - drous sight. The an - gels shone bright - ly
in the sky, a mes - sage they did bring, "Glo - ry to the
new - born King. Come fol - low the
star, it will guide you to Beth - le - hem.
CHORUS
Simon / Scott / Patrick, Maracas

Em7   Am7   D
Come fol-low the star   and   see the new
G   G7   Cadd9   C
King.   He's wrapped in a   swad-dling tight,
Cm   G
on a ve-ry cold Christ-mas night.   Come fol-low the
Am7   D   D7   G
star,   come see the new King."
cresc.

Am   D   mf G   Em7
2. Wise men they came to Beth - le - hem, the

Am   D7   Am   D7
bright star was their guide. They brought with them some pre - cious gifts and

G   D7   Em
laid them by His side. The an - gels shone bright - ly

Am
all a - round, their prais - es they did sing,

A
A7
Am7add4
f
cresc.
"Glo - ry to the new - born King.____
D //
CHORUS mf
Am7
D
Come fol - low the star, it will guide you to
mf
G6
Em7
Am
Beth - le - hem.____ Come fol - low the star
D
G
G7
and see the new King. He's wrapped in a

Cadd9
C
Cm
G
swad - dling tight,
on a ve - ry cold Christ - mas night.
Am7
D
f
Come fol - low the star,
come see the new
To sustain the lower part, note G for "King" – each
singer takes a breath at a different point.
The tone and volume will then be maintained.
Tomb + Marrcas
G
div.
Am7
The new - born King.
mf
G
f King."
f
cresc.
Fadd2
The new - born King."
mf rit.
G
f
f
rit.
ff
ff